Paper Radio

Paper Radio

Poems by Damian Rogers

MISFIT

ECW Press

Published by ECW Press, 2120 Queen Street East, Suite 200
Toronto, Ontario, Canada   M4E 1E2
416.694.3348 / info@ecwpress.com

NATIONAL LIBRARY OF CANADA CATALOGING IN PUBLICATION DATA

Rogers, Damian, 1972–

Rogers, Damian
Paper radio / Damian Rogers.

Poems.
"A misFit book".
ISBN 978-1-55022-892-2

I. Title.

PS8635.O425P36 2009   C811'.6   C2009-902536-1

Editor for the Press: Michael Holmes / a misFit book
Cover and text design: Adam Harris
Author photo: John Goodhew
Typesetting: Gail Nina
Printing: Coach House Press   2   3   4   5

The publication of *Paper Radio* has been generously supported by the Canada Council for the
Arts, which last year invested $20.1 million in writing and publishing throughout Canada, by
the Ontario Arts Council, by the Government of Ontario through Ontario Book Publishing
Tax Credit, by the OMDC Book Fund, an initiative of the Ontario Media Development
Corporation, and by the Government of Canada through the Book Publishing
Industry Development Program (BPIDP).

ECW PRESS
ecwpress.com

For Michael and Jo

Just because a thing can never be finished
doesn't mean it can't be done.
— Dean Young

The Suicide Seat

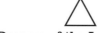

Dreams of the Last Shaker

Red Thread

The Suicide Seat

I really love you.
And I mean you.
— Syd Barrett

Redbird

It's the middle of the night.
I've set the house on fire
with those matches I love,
the ones in the kitchen
with the red bird on the box.
You can strike them anywhere.
Allumettes qui s'allument partout.
Take care: may ignite if box is
dropped, shaken, or crushed.
This same bird flies through
a tattoo on your arm.
The house is burning down
and I am thinking of boats.
You hate the matches, the smell
of bent, black spoons.
I light one and it falls to the floor.
Another and another. Take care.
I don't know what to save
from this place, sailing from wall
to wall, room to room, smoking.
You are not here. You are rain
battering against some window.
I don't know what to save.
The red bird eats everything in sight.

Sleeping Till Ten

I woke up today and thought about myself
as if it were my happiest birthday.

Every day there are new stores.
They look so shiny and great,
mouths stuffed with presents.

I am calculating exactly how much they owe
me and wondering if I can be paid in toys.

I dreamed I swallowed an anchor and sunk
to the bottom of a bottomless sea.
I was wearing spectacular, red-feathered shoes.

Please understand that I want to be good.

Found Weather

I feel convinced that the world will not come to an end.

Of course, there are exceptions.

It could be so easy on you.

We clandestinely acquired three of the scrolls
from a Christian Arab antiquities dealer in Bethlehem.

Our scientists are worrying about the exclusively negative
and possibly lethal uses of their various special discoveries.

His idea was to attract the electricity
from the lightbulb with the metal hanger
and transmit it through his body to the plant.

He accepted chance and weather as the country did,
with a sort of grave enjoyment.

I was rushing along a pitch-black tunnel, but a voice said,
Go back, we don't want you yet.

This, then, was the way it all began many years ago
in the middle of this vast continent.

I was self-appointed inspector of snowstorms
and rainstorms, and did my duty faithfully.

This post is now open.

The Brass Bell

Cocteau's Beauty glides
in silver-screen brilliance
down a river of light.

It's a trick. Her ball gown conceals
roller skates. An off-camera push
and she floats along singing.

Her face a stretched canvas,
she's an ancient fetish doll,
all tits and womb.

The way I remember it,
her voice is a brass bell ringing,

a voice high enough to change
the shape of the human body,
to fill the cupboards with apples.

Your bed vibrates with the secrets
you keep sealed inside your skin.

A GREAT HAPPINESS AWAITS

A young girl rides a bike
down a brushstroke road,
gravel biting her ankles.
The smell of an orchard in bloom
hits her in the chest
like an open hand.

Let's sing with the girl
as her feet spin out a sustained
whole note: O . . . .

It's simple. She loves a man
who is married to another,
one who wishes that she dry up
and crumble like an autumn leaf.

It's simple. There will be plums.
There will be a white pillow beneath her head.
There will be things worth writing down.

HARD WATER

I'm beginning to think God
is a cold pool in Tucson
surrounded by red doors.

Send me a signal, my body
an underwater antenna
tuned to a black line of tile.

Send me a sign: a coyote
in the courtyard, or three flying
objects leapfrogging the moon.

I swim in the dark
and the night
rings nine chimes.

The space between the water
and my skin is the distance
separating me from you.

HER TEETH

In sleep, she grinds her teeth into flour.

Her teeth are boiled plums.

Her teeth are a string of stones.

Her teeth eat meat, chew liver, chew onion.

Her teeth are a Greek amphitheatre.

Her teeth are a grandstand band.

Her teeth are singular. Her teeth are plural.

Her teeth keep her up all night with their questions.

Her teeth love gossip, are careless and cruel and given to rages.

Her teeth lie around and wait for you to turn 18.

Her teeth summer where they winter.

Her teeth think you could do something better with your life.

Her teeth call your mother and tell her everything.

Her teeth stay out past dawn.

Her teeth invite the Weather Underground into the house
    and let them use the phone.

Her teeth hitchhike to Nunavut without leaving a note.

Her teeth mean well. Her teeth mean nothing.

Her teeth break all her promises.

Her teeth bite down on the last word.

Her teeth fall out and scatter like change.

Her teeth roll under the couch and sleep in beds of lint.

Her teeth leap into every beautiful mouth they see.

New House

The phone breaks down
and the world breaks down with it,
coiled cable for good news
now a limp snake on the floor.

The sky offers us nothing except
the abstraction of memory,
the illusion we call blue.
It's one of those perfect clear days
when sunlight moves without challenge.

See how wind weaves through the trees,
how shadows play the yard like a typewriter,
branches tapping lines out across the grass
that no one bothers to read.

Code everywhere.

The table is covered in cut flowers,
potted lemon balm, a dead woman's mail.
Everything we own packed up like gifts
we picked out for ourselves.

JUNK MAIL

Marie Antoinette stands in line at a soup kitchen.
It would be great if there were enough for everyone.

You, for one, have been in denial your whole life.
Press play and record at the same time, then rewind.

I'm sorry that you were born without rubies,
but that hardly ensures the nobility of your enterprise.

We've all been caught stealing
from the lost and found.

The public gardens are filthy with imaginary toads
and I just want to fool around in that field.

You've been ringing my doorbell all night,
pockets stuffed with someone else's letters.

MUSEUM OF TOMORROW

Men kick a small sphere in the grass, laughing.
They have no cares. They carelessly
drop wedding rings, currency, poison darts.
Blank pages fly among their hands.

The future is unwritten.
It's a sleeping fox,
his cold back
concealing the next act.

The sun bears down on the crown of the heads
of those awake in the heat of the day.
Their monument grows pale, its shadow thin.
This is ours, and not ours. Pass it on.

ONE LIE

I'm so glad you called.

Your problem is my problem,
which is why I hate hearing about it.

Today was cold for October 13.
I walked through the neighborhood
and into the next one, past trees
that shook their many, many hands
as if to say, You know what happens next.
I stood before a bust of Simón Bolívar.
His eyes were surprisingly kind
as they surveyed the parkette.
He has been there since 1983.

The shops were full of dead people's things;
waves and waves of once-loved stuff
cast away and then rescued from worthlessness.
Hat boxes, souvenir shrimp forks, Duran Duran pins.
I once had a white satin tie, the Union Jack
silk-screened off-centre at the bottom.
It was on sale; I remember its ink stain.
I wore it thinking of a New Romantic bass player,
whose cheekbone-length bangs were bleached brass,
the colour of a button on an Army Navy Surplus coat.

Too much coffee, then tea, then *Scary Monsters* on vinyl.
The first time I met my father it might have been 1983.
Maybe as we awkwardly faced off over a long table
in the chlorinated halls of that YMCA in southern Michigan,
Caracas was sending a commemorative bust to Toronto.
But really, now that I do the math, it was probably 1985.
I might have been wearing a Duran Duran pin
on my cheap navy sweatsuit that had PIRANAHAS
hand-stitched in gold thread down one arm.
(The spelling a mistake not worth fixing.)

And you called me this afternoon after a night of bad things,
you who were born not long into Reagan's first term,
because you woke up hating yourself and thought of me.

POOR JANE

Out on the rented clover
I was thinking how Russian aristocrats
seemed to spend a lot of time

hanging out at each other's houses.
Revolutionaries shot the bad people
only to fire up the endless business

of being bad people. Is it so hard
to stop thinking of others?
They say if I wait long enough

a guard will get in my way.
We see the outline of our character
only as it slips out the back door

and returns like a challenging houseguest,
the kind who claims a favorite mug,
turns your office into a foreign apartment.

They've made instant versions
of foods that were already easy:
popcorn, oatmeal, noodle soup.

There are dials on at least one object
in every room, but I can't tune you out.
I wonder what you've heard.

Song of the Silver-Haired Hippie

When the old farmhouse has fallen down
And all the grass has turned to brown
Money comes to me

When black ice is on the ground
And the night's sucked clean of sound
Money comes to me

Glory, how I love this town
Though rivals rise from every bow
With their eyes fixed on my crown
O, Money, come to me

BETTER LIVING THROUGH INDUSTRY

Procrastination is the
art of keeping
up with yesterday
            — Don Marquis

Learn from Norma Desmond's broken ego:
her Baroque delusion displayed in lace shades
that shower her bedroom with the light of forgiveness
while rats scratch around in the dried-up pool
out back. Yet her face never creases inside her
projector — beauty only survives in an image.

We should know. We're a chorus
of crones, come to take inventory,
to point out the facts of your indolence.

A procession of pecan trees in an unhung photograph,
two bags of quince rotting in the cold room,
a thick layer of last year coating the floorboards:
your cozy home trapped in a state of later
while you sit and watch old movies on TV.

The history of our resistance is kept in cookbooks
collected from communes long since closed:
recipes for Fancy Persian Rice and Mushroom Pie
paired with quotes from Emerson's essays, photographic
still-lifes of the North American Bohemian Habitat,

complete with cat, guitar, houseplant, and cast-iron
cookware. You see domestic bliss in the liner notes
of a lesser-known Neil Young album, all yellowed edges
and sepia-toned scenes set in autumn, on an afternoon
where the leaves glow like gold and prepare their fall.

We've documented all your unfinished business,
the long to-do you've still not done: a novel called
Notes from the Suicide Seat, a screenplay named
The Last Night of the Party . . . we could go on.

Look, life is like a romance novel
with the last chapter ripped out,
all hot promise and complication
without the surrender that signals
desire's dead end.

This is it.

We live in your hands.
Keep them moving.

IN THE BACK OF A CAB

I lean my body against the door
of a car I'll never ride in again.

In the long line of stores and restaurants
I'll never visit, your name blinks
on a sign that says it has your pizza.
I've never found my name
on any sign, in any city.

So many people move around me,
invisible within the labyrinths
of skyscraper and subway.
They can't know how I planned to save us all
with the secret of human happiness,
which just this morning
I held in my hand like a rock.

But today was too long —
now all I remember is
a few lines from a song,
something about 20,000 roads,
how they all lead back to me,
here, alone in a stranger's car

in the middle of the night,
secretly hoping the driver,
who politely pretends I don't exist,
would devote the rest of his life
to taking me home.

Running Along Ontario

1.
Winter

My body is too much work in this weather,
movement requiring an effort that suggests
unreasonable expectations.

When you first brought me here, you ran ahead,
pointing to horseshoe prints in the snow.

You followed the tracks and I followed you,
until the shape of each U began to dissolve,
like luck seeping out into the cold.

In my grandparents' house, my mother slept in the basement.
California had released her from its relentless glare,
        pregnant and alone.

I'd sit on the stair and listen to her talk to herself,
reciting arguments she'd lost, worrying over them
until they were smooth stones.

I hold my bitterness like this too.
I've spent months at the bottom of the house,
pills keeping me afloat on our enormous bed.

At the lake, evergreens take on a new authority
as they refuse to let go of their needles.

The pine's lank arms sweep the ground,
creating a tent around the trunk.
I lift a branch and crawl in.

My breath builds small birds in the air that vanish
almost as quickly as they escape from my mouth.

This is how we will fly out of our bodies when we die.

2.
Spring

I have a gift for crying, a talent I'm wired for.
My mother falls apart during long-distance commercials
in which estranged family members finally connect.

When I run, it's as if a rusted lock has unlatched.
My feet lose their rhythm on the pavement.

Days ago, at the health food store,
I sat on bags of rice with my face in my hands.
A stock boy knocked nervously on the locked door.
Are you hurt? Do you need a doctor?

Most of the lake ice has melted and driftwood stacks up.

A whole tree trunk rolls back and forth in the shallows
like the body of a woman floating on her back.
I want to drag it out of the water and take it home.

Two swans stand like sentries at the water's edge,
their feathers the color of tobacco stains.

My socks are sopping wet. With each step I jam more mud
into the grooves of my overpriced shoes.

I remember a dream of whales beaching their bodies on sand
like men tossing themselves off bridges or buildings.
As if death were as simple as surrendering to another element.

When the path turns back to blacktop,
I see a couple smoking du Mauriers,
holding each other up.

The lake turns back on itself endlessly.

3.
Summer

One cat in the grey urn on the mantel,
the other trying to get out the back door.
She cases sparrows through the window, biding her time.

I hold this picture of her in my mind as I run to the end of the city,
her body's compact outline framed by geraniums.

In this light, Lake Ontario is gold-flecked lapis,
the robes of the Madonna spread out at my feet.
I imagine myself dragging my shadow across it.

Water flows from the taps.
I drain the lake one glass at a time.

Years ago, on my way into surgery, I repeated this mantra:
Rainwater on tomatoes, rainwater on tomatoes . . .

The power has gone out on the right side of the country,
the whole coast now quiet and still.

At home, I've let weeds choke the backyard,
morning glories losing all sense of time,
blowing their trumpets all day long.

Love takes on the taste of chalk,
of aspirin stuck in the throat.

Days have disappeared, my vision a television blur.
The outdoors hurts my eyes.

At the wedding party I drank until I hated you and left alone.
The cab driver asked me why I was crying.
He offered me a joint and told me about Ghana.

I retain nothing.

As a child, my mother read my Tarot cards,
insisting fortune can always be changed.

I'm sweating, my face burns. I want to stop.
I'm thirsty.

I'm Scarlet — *Tomorrow*,
I promise everyone,
Tomorrow.

4.
Fall

Time divides like cells into weekdays and hourly appointments.

Monarchs follow me as I run to the lake.
It's cold. Their batteries are running out.

Last night, my eyes were blindfolded. I held a sword in each hand.

Once, a man asked me if my eyes changed colour like the lake.
Then he told me he loved me. I laughed at him.
We were strangers.

The moon is gold-green and I sleep again.

How could we have known we would survive like this?
In a time when trees are ripped out of the ground like carrots
and rooftops snap right off houses.

It's hurricane season.
The ocean throws its weight around, refusing to stay in its bed.
I'm grateful the lake calmly maintains its borders.

The kitchen knives smell of fresh ginger and garlic.
We protect our good health.
You promise me that everything will be okay.

I believe you.

I run along the lake that's named for its beauty,
breathing without pain.

The world has no corners,
though everything we build in it does.

Dreams Of
The Last Shaker

I can only give you everything.
— MC5

The Family

Welcome.

Your name was written in our book
years before you found us.

Lonely child, see the gallery
where photographs of your face smile
in various stages of development
beside your brothers and sisters.

Go ahead, pledge yourself to the world.
You have always belonged to us.

Stubborn climber of invisible trees,
little one who runs.

We watched you wheel your possessions
from city to city, searching for strong walls.

We saw our children battle over china plates
and the fine tines of silver forks.

We speak from the line
where the desert rises, resettles.
Our beaded dress, our braided belt,
our string of pearls, all gone.

Above us, a red bird
crosses a blue sky.

Look at the light at your feet.
The sun is the only gold we need.

MILK AND HONEY

A cardinal flits through the branches
and the bush appears to burn.

Who are we to say we were thrown out?

We fell asleep,
the garden withered.

We turned our eyes inward
toward our dearest lies.

After weeks of late snow
last year's daffodils shove up
beside blue and white hyacinths.

The grass is so green it's shocking.

This may or may
not be true:

I'm only here
to sing for you.

Snake Handler

No tricks,
I just love them
as my own blood

and keep my eyes
on the ceiling.

O Brothers, I sing,
your bodies are thick

as wrists, your skins
my only book.

I relieve them
of poison,

I undo what they do.
I'm charcoal and paper.

Touch me: I leave
a mark on your hand.

This is just costume,
my Depression dress,
my buckled shoe.

Tin flowers in my ears
play spiral-groove blues.

Prayer Lesson

Martha, open me.
Empty me.
Fill me with your love.

Open me like a music box.
Empty me of my worn-out springs.
Fill me with "The Ballad of John and Yoko."

Open me like a hatchback.
Empty me of all these rain-beaten scissors.
Fill me with the light of your basement.

Open me like a chestnut.
Empty me of piano keys.
Fill me with homemade apple butter.

Martha, open me.
Empty me.
Fill me with Martha.

PROBLEMS WITH ANIMALS

The swans don't speak the same language.

The elephants are furious with us.

The apes are jealous and play mind games with our women.

The bears have grown too fond of potato chips.

The whales are on welfare.

The fish are on meth.

The cats are skimming off the top.

The wolves are hiding the silverware.

The coral has bad taste in music.

The mice won't stop setting small fires.

The giraffes are blocking the intersection.

The horses have developed eating disorders.

The rats have been stealing our jewelry.

The tigers have low self-esteem.

The penguins are weak-willed and spend their days preening.

The bats demand to be driven downtown.

The dogs have called a press conference
to publicly announce they were wrong about us.

ANOTHER POEM FOR WARNER STRINGFELLOW

Stay tuned to the paper radio for more news as it happens.
— John Sinclair

I hate the pigs, said the kids.
And the crimes of my skin.

We've forgotten the daughter
slaughtered by her father,
gunned down in her sleep
on Lincoln Street, naked
in bed with her sweetheart

and some of his friends. Later,
the papers were pointed about a black boy
crashed out on a couch in the next room,
wiped out with the rest.

Four dead in Detroit City.

We understand!
                cried the parents.
Kill the assassin!
                cried the pacifists.

The young ones plotted to blot out their families
in a mushroom cloud of dope smoke and dancing.
They demanded free music in municipal parks.
They dressed in their weedhead best, spent days
beading bracelets, quoting Minh and Mao and Marx.

They thought love would lead them
into a rainbow-domed freedom
from men who believed children
were a form of property.

These days, it's hard to say
how the news broke through back
then, we only know hatred circulated
among the citizens like contagion.

And still the pretty babies lined
up outside the People's Ballroom,
their legs dipped in psychedelic
stockings. There were whispers
about so-and-so's sister, the one
who made it with a Temptation.

They swore the sun was setting on the West,
that they were free, mother-country maniacs.

They declared war on the way it was,
divided the living into discreet districts:
over there, control-addict creeps;
over here, street-fucking freaks.

In time, their embroidered banners
gave way to racks of designer jeans.
They traded the city for a patch
of grass the size of a stamp.

They collected their wits while
they sang without thinking —

Our sons
will never
burn out.

Sun Down

They have formed committees to examine why
the sky has been torn from the horizon.
In quick consensus, they blamed our enemies.

But several feral scientists have released statements
from the safety of their bachelor apartments
claiming the sun was simply sick of us

clinging to her skirts and pulling
at her hair. She's lost interest
in our litany of childhood abuse.

So they locked you in a closet.
So they burned down your dollhouse.
So they stole your horses

and swallowed the yellow moon
you grip in your fist in your sleep.
Open your eyes; you are dreaming.

The planet's in pieces, Borneo's jungle
reduced to a jingle of coins locked
in exotic boxes made from sacred shade

and I have blood on my clothes
from killing a creature
that turned out not to be harmless.

In Russia, a man weeps with pleasure
as his shovel uncovers the bones
of his country's could-have-been,

preteen crown prince whose bloodline
was bashed out by the Bolshies in one-nine
one-eight. And why should he care if

our lights are snuffed out?
In the end, every child
will be a czar of the dead.

Just because the future is unwritten
doesn't mean that it's unplanned.
The tear up there is nothing new.

FORTUNE, TELL HER

1.

Agamemnon is a fish in a plastic bowl,
he is a bald man, a spent man, a tired old
tax man. His royal robes dust the marble
as he staggers his way to his last bath.

The fabric drapes in folds
like the skin on his face
and the flesh at his waist.

He sinks into his imperial pool
and then blossoms like a rose
under his wife's pruning tools.

He knows he's been thrown over-
board. He remembers the whore
he stole, her body untouched except
by God's pen, a deep blue birthmark
on her neck: a curl, a question.

2.

*Things don't look good from
here*, Cassandra thinks as she peers
down a dark hall lit by the milk
in her breasts; pink moons; camp

lanterns illuminating a hidden room.
She sees how a war finds its way home.

To feel the blade before it falls
is to be captured in perpetual
tragedy. She repeats her lines
ten thousand times: *No,
don't make me go*.

The chorus coughs
and studies their nails.

The world as we know it is
forever coming to a close.
She was His, then his,
but never her own.

Autobiography

She wants to
be a haughty old
woman, a high-
boned bitch.

Prideful, angular.
Spine-straight,
flat-lapped.

She wants to
wear work
shirts, be
blunt-haired
and sharp-
tongued.

She wants
to press
her final
breath

into the
corners
of every
room she
enters.

Dream of the Last Shaker

We stream into the meetinghouse
through two doors

like twin cords
in the same braid.

I love the men,
all of them

lined up like
God's long finger.

The sun attends everything
equally: the wood, the bend

of her white muslin sleeve,
the outstretched arm of the apocalypse.

Take hold of my shoulder.
Shake me awake.

The Era of Manifestations

The sky was red
My dress was red
Mother came to me in bed

She wrapped me in linen
She wrapped me in wool
Her hands on my head
were like two cool stones

The sky was white
My dress was white
She cut my sins out with her knife

She held me under
She lifted me up
She ladled me into
her favourite cup

She drew a tree within the air
She brushed a song upon my lip
She packed me with pictures
and music like prayer, then dropped
me dancing on the stair

The sky is blue
My dress is too
She uses me
to get to you

The Hole

Heal me
of this small
black stone.

Eat it up
and leave
me whole.

CHARITY

I see your body buried
under fifteen yards of cotton,
arms slight as snakes.

You don't eat. You pass out pie,
each plate a punch card.
You're never not working.

You long to lift off the ground
but I've tracked your prints
in the dust behind the barn.

I trail your movements, less like
a shadow, more like a man.
I stand in your wake, close as I can.

At night I dream how your hip
would melt like a snowbank
under the heat of my hand.

Song of the Last Shaker

One line,

        two line,

                three line,

                        plane.

I skate across the lake on a bone-made blade.

My spine is an arrow, a leg of His chair.

My nose straight and narrow and long
                as my hair.

My body's for bruising.

My heart is her sky.

I train my breath
      upwards.

I practice.

I die.

Death of the Last Shaker

Horses tear
through my skin,

racing to meet what
has not yet happened.

They seek any
hole that will

open to hold me.
They find one in you.

There are endings everywhere
our bodies take us.

THE END

I thought it would be beautiful.

My heart sewn up like a suit.

I thought it would be beautiful.

A stream of light shot through the wall.

I thought it would be beautiful.

I thought it would be you.

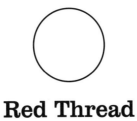

Red Thread

The glacier knocks in the cupboard,
The desert sighs in the bed,
And the crack in the tea-cup opens
A lane to the land of the dead.
— W. H. Auden

KEYS

The blue box-van was filled with keys —
your brother was a locksmith then,
but he never broke into me.

His wife won ten grand in the lottery
and took a long trip to Japan
while the blue box-van was filled with keys.

His days were short and dark and free.
He broke into houses again and again,
but he never broke into me.

The alcohol was called a disease,
but they looked away too much back when
the blue box-van was filled with keys.

His arms were tattooed when he was at sea:
a panther, a dragon, three anchors in pen.
He never broke into me.

I saw my fear in a shadow's teeth
though I only half-knew the dangers of men.
The blue box-van was filled with keys,
but he never broke into me.

THE GREAT ERASE

1.
Fall exploded in a round of arson,
maples burning back to the branch.
It was time to leave town.

2.
Winter bleached the sky grey
except for flashes of blue jay and cardinal.

The jays bullied the sparrows,
eating their drab little eggs,

but a red bird in the yard
meant a kiss was coming.

3.
The earth swelled with rain,
smelling like wet leaves,
turned ground, teenage sex.

I rolled down the window for air.

We drove back and forth
between our parents' houses.

4.
One minute it's Endless Summer,
then it's time to turn on the furnace.

Soon, I'll leave all this behind.
I'm serious.

Biography

This is not my story.
Odds are good it's not yours either.

Though you never know
where your story will end up;
it might as well be here,
in some stranger's book.

A girl dials a number on a phone
shaped like a high-heeled shoe,
then hangs up before it rings through.

In another room, a glass of cream sherry
sits on a velvet tablecloth, on a stage
set with noisy wallpaper. Let's pipe in
the smell of bread baking in the oven
for a woman of a certain age watching
the story of George Sand on PBS.

A cramped blue-tiled kitchen radiates heat.
In the backyard there's a birdbath, grape arbor,
tree full of apples gathered in a pale green storm.

In a child's earliest recorded image,
we see a mother's legs on a ladder
as her arms vanish into the leaves.

Drugs for Girls

1.
we'll water the lawn barefoot
passing notes without using our hands
the key to the city is in the sun
so lie down and learn something
we ride the same wavelength
right through his rapacious brain
so let's be as pretty as possible
if we can sparkle he may land tonight

2.
I cover my face in silver paint
so I might return everything I see
I've lived all over the world, I've left every place
pyramid winds and diamond rains slaking the sphinx
a snooze — a unified indigo aura builds behind
our artificial curls under the glow of a black-light poster
watch as I move in imperfect time beneath
a crack in the sky and a hand reaching down to me

Honour Roll Student Drunk at Pep Rally

I know what you think, and for once I don't care.
Skipping class to pound rum and cokes at my house
puts these cheers in a whole new light: Go Blue.

Let's get out of here. I'll drive.

Let's not worry about where we're going
or how fast. Look honey, it's not rocket science.

Let's park your Corvair behind a Dumpster at Meijer's
and spend the rest of the afternoon drinking PBR.
Roll a joint and take down that feathered roach clip
hanging from your rearview mirror.

Let me have your tongue in my mouth for a while.
And for fuck's sake, stop talking.

I want to stay out until the night past the dashboard
is black as the cheap kohl eyeliner
I see the girls behind Sunshine Foods
melt down with their yellow lighters
before rimming their lids like rabid animals.

Come on, let's board up the windows with our breath.

Let your fingers slide inside my panties,
your belt buckle break open easily in my hands.

DON'T LOOK

It's like when you eat sour candy,
how the sugar-coated acid
twists your tongue into a knot.

At the Ambassador Roller Rink
no one would slow-skate with me.

A boy rolled over to you during the power ballad
and I turned into a pillar of salt.

No, that's wrong. I mean, I felt a lot like a sand dune. Or like
that baby food jar our family member filled with volcanic ash.

I asked the DJ to help me prove I knew the secret moves
for transforming my body into four different letters —

Y: raise your hands to the sky.
M: touch your shoulders like a mountain range.
C: pull your belly toward the door.
A: place your palms over your head and pray.

He said no. He said we don't play that song.

I said oh. I said wait, hold on;
I am changing into someone
completely different and better.

Hamilton Elementary

For M.

It's Devil's Night, the city is burning,
and here you are tossing TP into the gym
teacher's tree. Snagged streamers of tissue
make you think of a monster movie.
You imagine a grief-stricken ghost bride
who stalks the block in her shredded dress.

Cue porch light, man yelling
like a dad at the end of the day.
You run, leaving your friends
to fend for your friends.

There's no way you'd break into the school
if I weren't the one writing this story.
But through the window you must go in your
corduroy floods and rainbow windbreaker.

You clamber into the art room,
over cupboards that contain the tools
of construction: white paste, mixed
paints, snub-nosed safety scissors.

You turn toward a shelf lined with class assignments
and an army of papier-maché projects stares you down;
one brown-haired angel with red wings and flagrant
halo suggests it's okay to play both sides.

It was not so long ago you walked these halls as one
of the crowd. This is where you learned to build a fortress
using the basic units of form: triangle, circle, square.
Now the linoleum floor may as well be the moon.

In this light, the musty-green concrete-block walls
look porous as a sponge in the sink. The water performs
a back bend in the drinking fountain, murmurs an odd
music you hear through the holes between your teeth.

You curl up in a coat cubby that smells of old milk
and bananas, under a stack of half-day nap mats.
Later there will be a woman with hair down to her ass
and glasses too big for her head. A woman in wool
plaid. A woman in thick socks with soft hands.

A Man on a Motorcycle

A man on a motorcycle stops in the street.
He takes off his helmet, you stare at your feet.

You're alone with a friend and your dolls at the curb,
so the lawns all roll down to hear every word.

It just goes to show you never know who you'll meet
when a man on a motorcycle stops in the street.

His face is a smudge but he knows your first name;
in his mouth it sounds like some new kind of game.

He mentions your mother, he smiles, then he leaves.
See the man on a motorcycle ride off down the street.

JO-JO'S TAROT: RODS

Cardinal cries to find she's alone.

           The sun sounds the alarm

and Crow's call cuts the morning in half.

           Her panic spreads through the trees like heat.

JO-JO'S TAROT: COINS

Cardinal, who lived only branch to branch,

      now scratches at the soil like a labourer.

She scatters seed as she searches

      for her lover's ochre-stained skull.

JO-JO'S TAROT: CUPS

Cardinal bends over the bath

        and sees her sister in the world below.

They lean in eye to eye

        and drink deeply from the well of the other.

JO-JO'S TAROT: SWORDS

Cardinal rows through the sky

        in a boat of red smoke.

Her song soars beyond her body, scaling a wall of sound.

        She can never catch up.

WE ARE THE DAUGHTERS OF THE AMERICAN REVOLUTION

This bed is the center of the known universe

    smothered in summer-weight quilts in forty shades of red

each one a flag to cover our hand as it rests on the center

    of our body, palming our coarse bush while we choose new
        roses

from seed catalogs: Bourbon Queen, Gipsy Boy, Duchess of
    Portland.

    We hate the way our stomach sags like a poorly made purse

spent as the elastic in the snagged nylon panties that jam our
    dresser drawers.

    See how that slip hangs limp and beige off the closet's
        doorknob:

one day our underwear stopped living beautiful lives of their own.

    We sleep in ignorance as our uterus is edged out by a tumour

the size and shape of the golden fruit that drop onto our son's
    Floridian lawn.

    Our children's lives have splintered like toothpicks,
        grandchildren strewn

across the continent, struck dead by lightning, addicted to cocaine,
    heroin.

    No one tells us the truth anymore and we're grateful

though the lies bore us to tears. There are things we did that we've
    denied

long enough to undo. We conspire in church basements, our
        hearts cut out

like paper doilies. We meet at buffet tables over miniature tuna-
    fish sandwiches

        and Sweet Ambrosia Salad — medley of canned fruit and
            marshmallow trapped

in red gelatin — where we join together the warring cults of mayo
    and Miracle Whip.

        We are the Daughters of the American Revolution, our
            breasts wrapped

with a double-wide blue-and-white ribbon that buckles under a
    field

        of soldiers we tracked down the dubious trail of marriage and
            death certificates.

Row upon row, we wear our own private graveyard of immaculate
    dead,

        men who died desperate deaths we'll never know; our
            beloved, brutal blood.

Cordiform

We remember what it was like
when the world unfolded like a map,
intricate as a Victorian valentine.

We also remember when the thought of the sun rising
made us feel like we were chewing aluminum foil.

We too imagined our lungs
filling with warm bathwater.

We rested in liminal spaces,
our bodies framed
by windows and doors.

We wanted to thank you
for painting our fingernails electric pink
while we lay dying in the hospital.

It was a lovely gesture.

We remember our last breath,
how we rattled like a toy as they told us we would,
and of course, what came after.

We've learned we can't live
in the seed and in the grain.

We carved a star in the driveway
to give you a sign.

Follow the cracks.

Astonish Me

The name that can be named
is not the eternal Name.

Embroidered red blanket,
nest of papers, great pile
of pillows.

I can't tell if you're sleeping.

I approach from an angle,
calling you Delta, a name you buried
in life, snipped out of the records.

Fourth letter of the Greek alphabet;
bright triangle; the river's fat lip.

*

"If there's a way to come
back as a ghost, I will."

Foxglove, borage bush,
birdbath, feeder.

I watch you wave bees out of your lap
like you're dismissing the servants.

When I think of your lap
I imagine an overturned bowl.

I am here and
you are distant.

*

"The passenger side is a suicide seat:
the driver will always protect himself."

Burgundy Bonneville, baby blue Parisienne,
your daughter's white Pinto.

We sit out back where you named two birds
Mr. and Mrs. Cardinal. We sip cups of weak tea.

You never forgave him for that accident
back in the sixties. You could've died.

I haven't driven a car in more than a decade.

*

What did I accomplish yesterday?
What can I manage today?

Scrub floorboards, finish curtains,
prepare casserole, go for swim.

You gave yourself a hernia
doing hundreds of sit-ups.

I follow you into the house.
I sleep for weeks.

*

"Even Jake the Plumber, he's the man I adore,
he had the nerve to tell me he's been married before."

Coral necklace, thunderbird pendant,
brass cross, ivory bracelet.

We sing pop songs from the twenties
and thirties and I handle your jewelry.

Your foot pumps the piano's pedal;
square-heeled T-strap, tan nylons.

You exist.

*

"If I get out of this hospital
I'm going to write."

*Joyce essay, Plath piece, ten tips
on recycling for* Woman's Day.

Ambition the red thread
that stitched us together.

I no longer know if
this is yours or mine.

*

"What did I accomplish?"

Typed letter.

"What can I manage?"

*Washed and set hair.
Got dressed.*

Your notebooks document
how long you held a pen.

I take your wedding ring
and your maiden name

and leave you the rest.

CONCEPTION

2.
There were boards nailed over the window
and not a slice of bread in the house.

She was hungry and he answered
the door holding a sandwich.

Something had happened to her head.
She couldn't remember.

Maybe their car crashed into a palm tree.
Maybe drugs had untuned the room.

There were wings, or the sensation
of wings beating against her face.

She slept beside her husband
who counted her every breath.

One day, sun bled through the old
Times he'd taped over the glass,

headlines about war defeated
by the good news of morning.

This was before she knew I was coming.

1.
I've heard death is a failure
to connect your start to your finish

like a snake unable
to eat its own tail

and I still can't draw a line
to divide what I was given
from what I brought with me.

Notes

"Found Weather" is a found poem and the sources of some of the lines have been lost. The first and second line I can no longer identify; the third line is taken from the collected lyrics of Joe Pernice 1995–2003; the fourth line is taken from an account of the acquisition of the Dead Sea Scrolls; the fifth line I can't identify; the sixth line is from *Popism: The Warhol Sixties* by Andy Warhol and Pat Hackett; the seventh line is from *Death Comes for the Archbishop* by Willa Cather, as excerpted in the book *Utopian Vistas: The Mabel Dodge Luhan House and the American Counterculture* by Lois Palken Rudnick; the eighth line is from *The Study and Practice of Astral Projection* by Robert Crookall; the ninth line is from *Book of the Hopi: The First Revelation of the Hopi's Historical and Religious World-View of Life* by Frank Waters; the tenth line is from *Civil Disobedience* by Henry David Thoreau. One of the unidentified lines is by Buckminster Fuller. The final line is my own.

In "Better Living Through Industry," the Don Marquis quote is taken from "certain maxims of archy" as it appears in his book *Archy and Mehitabel*. The film in question is *Sunset Boulevard*.

In "Museum of Tomorrow," I lifted the line "The future is unwritten" off of a pin (for The Clash) that belonged to my husband when he was a teenager. (I echo the lines again in the poem "Sun Down.") "Museum of Tomorrow" was written in response to Mark Strand's poem "Letter," which originally appeared in his collection *Darker* (1970).

"In the Back of a Cab" cribs some phrasing from Gram Parsons' song "Return of the Grievous Angel."

The song "I Can Only Give You Everything" quoted at the opening of the "Dreams of the Last Shaker" sequence was written by Van Morrison when he was in the band Them, but it is the version by Detroit-based band the MC5 that I am referencing here.

"Snake Handler" was inspired by a drawing by Chicago artist Teresa Mucha.

Warner Stringfellow was a Detroit-area police officer who, during the late 1960s, had multiple run-ins with Detroit-area poet and activist John Sinclair. The manager of the MC5 and founder of the radical political group the White Panther Party, Sinclair wrote a poem called "A Poem for Warner Stringfellow" after facing drug charges in 1966. My poem also references a multiple homicide that happened in Detroit in 1968.

"Autobiography" was written in response to Robert Creeley's performance of his poem "Self-Portrait" as filmed by Ron Mann in 1981 for the documentary *Poetry in Motion*. The poem appears in Creeley's collection *Mirrors* (1981).

The Shakers were a religious group founded by Ann Lee, a factory worker and mother of five children who all died, in the late eighteenth century in Northern England. The group called themselves the United Society of Believers, though outsiders dubbed them "Shaking Quakers" or "Shakers" due to their practice of ecstatic dance during worship. Lee — or "Mother Ann," as she came to be known — sailed with a handful of followers to the United States in 1774 to avoid persecution. Once established in the States, the group grew and spread as far west as Kentucky, living in communal families on highly productive farms. The Shakers flourished in the mid-nineteenth century and at one time were considered the most prosperous and successful utopian experiment of its kind in North America. The Shakers practiced celibacy and essentially died out by the late twentieth century, though there are a handful of surviving elders. The Shakers are known today primarily for the clean lines of their furniture and architecture. The Last Shaker is a fictional character, as are many of her friends in this book.

"The Era of Manifestations" refers to a period in Shaker history from the late 1830s to the 1850s when a phenomenon emerged where young girls would enter into trance states during which they said Mother Ann, who had died in 1784, appeared to them in visions. They would often create what they called "Gift Drawings" and "Gift Songs" in the wake of these experiences.

In "Drugs for Girls," the third and final lines in both stanzas are taken from the following David Bowie songs, in order: "Eight Line Poem" from *Hunky Dory*; "Starman" from *The Rise and Fall of Ziggy Stardust and the Spiders From Mars*; "Be My Wife" from *Low*; and "Oh! You Pretty Things," also from *Hunky Dory*. Thanks to Matthew Rohrer for the form.

The poem "Cordiform" refers to a heart-shaped map of the world made in France in the sixteenth century.

The poem "Astonish Me" was inspired by the following sentence in Sigmund Freud's *Totem and Taboo*: "The living did not feel safe from the attacks of the dead till there was a sheet of water between them." The first line is taken from Stephen Mitchell's translation of the *Tao Te Ching*. The lines "Even Jake the Plumber, he's the man I adore / he had the nerve to tell me he's been married before" are from the 1921 song "Second Hand Rose (From Second Avenue)," written by Grant Clarke and James F. Hanley and originally sung by Fanny Brice. Barbra Streisand covered the song in the 1968 movie *Funny Girl*. The quoted lines are in the voice my maternal grandmother, Jeanne Rogers Shaffer (born Delta Jeanne Rogers), and the other lines in italics (with the exception of the poem's first line, noted above) are excerpts from her notebooks.

Acknowledgements

Thanks to Michael Holmes and everyone at ECW Press for making this manifest. Thanks to Adam Harris, kick-ass designer and believer in a better world, for making it look so good.

Some of these poems have appeared (often in slightly different form) in the following publications:

"Redbird," "In the Back of a Cab," "Honour Roll Student Drunk at Pep Rally," and "Cordiform" in *Brick Magazine*
"Death of the Last Shaker" (as "Our Bodies Take Us") in *Salt Hill*
"Dream of the Last Shaker" in *The Walrus*
"Poor Jane" and "Keys" in *MoonLit*
"Junk Mail," "Museum of Tomorrow," and "Conception" in *This Magazine*
"A Great Happiness Awaits," "Don't Look" and "Song of the Silver-Haired Hippie" in *Maisonneuve*

Many thanks to the respective editors.

"The Family" was read as part of the radio documentary *Journey of the Red Bird* on the CBC's *Outfront* in 2008.

Thanks to my teachers Lynda Barry, April Bernard, Henri Cole, Ken Mikolowski, Liam Rector (1947–2007), and Jason Shinder (1955–2008).

Thanks to Kevin Connolly and Matthew Zapruder — two of my favourite poets — for their indispensable encouragement and support.

Thanks to John Goodhew and John Taccone for the photo. Thanks to Kate Boothman and Sunbear for the warmest wintry nights at Graffiti's in Kensington Market, where many of these poems were first read out loud. Thanks to Emily Schultz for her sharp eyes and sensitive mind. Thanks also to Gil Adamson; Joanna Armstrong and the Shaffer family; Michael Belitsky and the Belitsky family;

Greg Keelor; Dan Koretzky; Joe Pernice; Michael Redhill; The Sadies collectively and Sean Dean, Dallas Good, and Travis Good individually; Amanda Schenk; Laura Stein; Joanne Tickle; Sally Timms; Heather Whinna; and Alana Wilcox for guidance, kindness, and inspiration during the creation of this book. Thanks to my whole family, through blood and through love.

This book was assisted by a grant from the Canada Council for the Arts and the Ontario Arts Council through its Writer's Reserve Program.